Families Share

Families share the chores.

Families share and play.

Families share a meal together
Every single day.

Families share the hard times.

Families share the fun.

Families share the work to do,

And families get it done!

Families Share

Families share the chores.
Families share and play.

Families share a meal together
Every single day.

Families share the hard times.
Families share the fun.

Families share the work to do,
And families get it done!